The entrance gateway of Preston Hall, Pathhead, Midlothian, with two Coade stone lions, c.1794.

Coade Stone

Hans van Lemmen

A Shire book

Published in 2006 by Shire Publications Ltd,
Cromwell House, Church Street, Princes Risborough,
Buckinghamshire HP27 9AA, UK.
(Website: www.shirebooks.co.uk)

Copyright © 2006 by Hans van Lemmen.
First published 2006.
Shire Album 453. ISBN-10: 0 7478 0644 6;
ISBN-13: 978 0 7478 0644 8.
Hans van Lemmen is hereby identified as the author of
this work in accordance with Section 77 of the Copyright,
Designs and Patents Act 1988.

British Library Cataloguing in Publication Data:
Lemmen, Hans van
Coade stone. – (Shire album; 453)
1. Coade stone 2. Stone carving – Great Britain – History –
19th century
3. Stone carving – Great Britain – History – 18th century
4. Decoration and ornament, Architectural – Great Britain –
History – 19th century
5. Decoration and ornament, Architectural – Great Britain –
History – 18th century
I. Title 729.6
ISBN-10: 0 7478 0644 6.

Cover: *The Coade stone lion on a pedestal at the Lambeth side of Westminster Bridge, London, designed by the sculptor W. F. Woodington, ARA, and dated 1837. It used to decorate the Lion Brewery on the South Bank and was saved when the brewery was demolished in 1951 to make way for buildings for the Festival of Britain.*

ACKNOWLEDGEMENTS
The author is grateful to the following people and institutions who have been of assistance
in the production of this book: Alison Copeland, Anna Hallett, Alison Kelly, Lynn Pearson,
John Rotheroe and Frances Voelcker. Photographs are acknowledged as follows: Anna
Hallett, page 26; Lynn Pearson, pages 27, 45 (bottom), 46; Manchester City Museums and
Art Galleries, page 21 (top); Cadbury Lamb, pages 3, 27 (top), 32 (bottom left), 40 (bottom),
41 (both), 42 (top), 47 (bottom). All other photographs are from the author's collection.

Printed in Great Britain by CIT Printing Services, Press Buildings,
Merlins Bridge, Haverfordwest, Pembrokeshire SA61 1XF.

Contents

Coade stone panel on the façade of Belmont, Throwley, Kent, 1792. The reclining woman represents Architecture. The building in low relief in the background is the house itself.

Mrs Eleanor Coade

Mrs Eleanor Coade was a well-known London businesswoman of her day and many reputable Georgian architects used the wide range of architectural terracotta products made at her factory in Lambeth. Her family came from Lyme Regis in Dorset, although she was born in 1733 in Exeter, where her father, George Coade, had settled to carry on a wool business. Her mother was also called Eleanor and this has at times caused some confusion as to who ran the Coade stone business. George Coade went bankrupt in 1759 and moved with his family to London, where he died in 1769. The same year the Coade stone business was set up at King's Arms Stairs, Narrow Wall, Lambeth, situated where the Royal Festival Hall now stands. It is not clear where the money for setting up this business came from, but the Coade family were Dissenters (nonconformists), who often supported one another financially, and so the family or other Dissenters may have invested in the venture.

To support herself and perhaps her family, Eleanor Coade ran her own linen and drapery business before the Coade factory was set up and must therefore have gained some financial experience in the process. Once the Coade factory was in operation bills were apparently paid to 'Miss

The doorway of Eleanor Coade's house, 'Belmont', in Lyme Regis, richly decorated with products of her own factory, 1784.

Coade', meaning that she rather than her mother ran the firm. Although she never married, Eleanor was known as 'Mrs' Coade – a courtesy title extended to unmarried businesswomen in Georgian times. She marketed her terracotta products as 'artificial stone' and its light creamy buff colour was designed to blend in perfectly with the stonework of Georgian architecture.

When the firm was first set up in 1769 Eleanor Coade went into a short-lived partnership with another artificial-stone manufacturer, Daniel Pincot. He no doubt supplied the practical experience that Eleanor must have lacked, as there is no record of her family being involved in any form of pottery production. The partnership ended acrimoniously in 1771, after which she ran the firm on her own under the name 'Coade'. At this time she engaged the services of the sculptor John Bacon (also a Dissenter), who not only provided artistic designs but also helped with the management of the business until his death in 1799. The Coade firm exhibited their best classical figures at the Society of Artists throughout the 1780s, and these were entered under the name 'Miss Eleanor Coade, sculptor' – which has led to the belief that she was also artistically involved in creating the firm's products. However, Georgian ideas about artistic ownership and copyright were very different from what they are today and she may have laid claim to these exhibits because they were the products of her firm.

Whatever her precise involvement as an artist, she did well as a businesswoman because in 1784 she was able to take over the lease on a large house, called Belmont, in Lyme Regis, which used to belong to her uncle Samuel Coade, and used it as a seaside retreat. In 1799 she was also able to build a special gallery near the Lambeth side of Westminster Bridge for the display of Coade products to prospective clients. In the

The factory mark used between 1769 and 1799, when Mrs Coade was the main proprietor, on the base of a keystone at Croome Park, Worcestershire.

The factory mark used between 1799 and 1813, when Mrs Coade was is in partnership with John Sealy, on the base of the tomb of Major General Bowes in Beverley Minster, East Yorkshire.

same year she went into partnership with her cousin John Sealy, who had already been working for the Coade firm before that date. He proved to be a successful partner as he was not only an able manager but also a good clay modeller and he helped with the firm's commissions. During their partnership the factory was known as 'Coade & Sealy'. After his death in 1813 the firm's name reverted to the earlier name 'Coade'.

By the time John Sealy died, Eleanor Coade was eighty years old and unable to run the business on her own, so she took on the young William Croggon, a distant relation, to manage the business for her, though she never made him a partner. When Eleanor Coade died in 1821 he bought the business and for a few years carried on under the name 'Croggon late Coade' and then as just plain 'Croggon'. After his death in 1835 his son Thomas John owned the business until the early 1840s, when he sold out.

The factory mark used by William Croggon after Mrs Coade's death in 1821, as seen on a statue of a hind on top of the entrance gateway to the Easton Neston estate at Towcester, Northamptonshire.

The factory mark used by Croggon after abandoning the name Coade, on the base of a Medici vase in Kew Gardens.

Eleanor Coade seems to have been an able businesswoman (perhaps also an artist) with an entrepreneurial spirit who with the right contacts and partnerships built up a successful business patronised by the wealthy upper echelons of society (including the King) and the foremost architects and sculptors of the day. When she died in 1821 she was known well enough to warrant an obituary notice in the *Gentleman's Magazine*; it read:

> November 18th at Camberwell in her 89th year, Mrs Eleanor Coade, sole inventor and proprietor of an art which deserves considerable notice. In 1769 a burnt artificial stone manufactory was erected by Mrs Coade at King's Arms Stairs, Narrow Wall, Lambeth. This manufactory has been carried on from that time to the present on a very extensive scale, being calculated to answer every purpose of stone carving, having a property peculiar to itself of resisting the frost and consequently of retaining that sharpness in which it excels every kind of stone sculpture and even equals marble itself.

Eleanor Coade was buried in Bunhill Fields cemetery, Finsbury, a special Dissenters' burial ground in London, not in a Coade stone tomb as one might have expected, but in the family tomb erected for her father before Coade stone tombs and gravestones were available. Although many graves can still be seen at Bunhill Fields cemetery today, the area where the Coade family tomb used to be was bombed during the Second World War and nothing remains there now.

8

Production techniques

Artificial stone was made before Mrs Coade came on to the scene in 1769. In 1722 Richard Holt took out a patent for making artificial stone but the patent was deliberately written in such vague language that its precise nature cannot be determined, although it seems to have been some kind of ceramic material that must have involved a heating process. He ran his business for a while in the same area of Lambeth where the Coade factory was later established. Other types of artificial stone, such as stucco and cement, were usually cast 'cold' but that made them susceptible to penetration by rain and frost damage. Coade stone, however, was a special composition of fired clay that was passed through the kiln at very high temperature, transforming it into a type of stoneware impervious to rain and frost.

Although Coade stone was marketed as 'artificial stone' it was sometimes referred to as 'Lythodipyra', which is based on the Greek meaning 'stone [*litho*] twice [*di*] fire [*pyra*]'. This name refers to the fact that already fired clay material, known as grog, was ground fine and mixed in with the unfired clay, together with flint, sand and ground glass. All this helped to reduce the rate of shrinkage during the drying and firing stages, and a controlled rate of shrinkage allowed for greater precision in determining the exact size of the products after they came out of the kiln, which was important to architects when planning their building designs.

A detail of a broken Coade stone statue of a druid in the grounds of Shugborough House, Staffordshire, showing that statues were made hollow.

The formula for Coade stone was never a secret, as has sometimes been claimed. The architect David Laing (1774–1856), who used Coade stone, described its composition in a book (1818) on his Custom House in London: '[Coade stone is] a material which, although composed of various ingredients, may be described as a species of terracotta. It combines in one mass, pipe-clay, flint, sand, glass and stoneware, that has already passed the furnace. These are ground to very fine powder, and are mixed in the proper proportions, and the whole is well kneaded together by means of the addition of water. In this state it forms a kind of paste which has the ductility of the clay usually employed in modelling.'

Coade stone products were made with the aid of plaster moulds. The object was first modelled in ordinary clay at a scale of 13 inches (330 mm) to the foot (305 mm), and from this model plaster moulds were made. The complexity of the form of the statue, vase or architectural ornament determined how many moulds would be needed. The carefully prepared Coade clay would be rolled into sheets about 3 to 4 inches (75 to 100 mm) thick, which would be pressed by hand into the plaster moulds, a process known as 'press moulding'. When the clay had dried to a state resembling leather it would have shrunk enough to be detached

Engraving of the interior of a Coade kiln illustrated in the 'European Magazine' of 1786. The caption at the bottom reads: 'A View of the River God THAMES 9 feet Figure & 4 SEASONS as placed in the kiln for Burning, so as to represent Stone, at the Lythodipyra at Lambeth.'

from the mould and the various sections were assembled. After assembly, the leather-hard clay was worked again to shape and undercut details and to smooth the joints, and then it was left to dry again. Coade stone statues made in this way were hollow; this was a necessary part of the manufacturing process, because large objects made of solid clay cannot be fired without cracking when they are in the kiln. The Coade pieces were fired in large muffle kilns, which had a refractory interior shell shielding the ware from the direct flames; the kiln interiors were big enough to accommodate complete statues.

Some interesting information about firing Coade products has survived in a letter from John Lygo, the London representative of the Derby porcelain factory, who in 1790 obtained information from a fireman in charge of the Coade kilns about their production processes. This letter, quoted in L. Jewitt's *The Ceramic Art of Great Britain* (1878), states:

> 'There is three kilns, the largest is 9 feet diameter and about 10 feet high… They make use of no saggers, but their kilns are all muffled about two inches thick, which was always done by this fire-man. They always was four days and four nights of fireing a kiln… He has been use to fire intirely with coal (which are call'd Hartley coals – they are not much unlike yours at Derby). He never made use of any thermometer, but depended intirely on his own knowledge. The composition shrinks about half an inch in a foot in the drying, and about the same in the firing. A great deal of the ornaments are 4 inches thick when fired, and he has fired figures 9 feet high. This man has had the intire management of building the kilns, setting and firing them for many years; his wages was one guinea per week and for every night when he fired he had 2s. 6d. for the small kiln, 3s. for the next size, and 3s. 6d. for the largest.'

The magnificent Coade stone statue of the river-god Thames by John Bacon in front of Ham House, Surrey.

Above left: *Statue of Ceres, the corn goddess, on the orangery at Burton Constable, East Yorkshire, made unsightly by layers of peeling paint.*

Above right: *Statue of a naiad (water nymph) in the entrance foyer of Shire Hall, Chelmsford, showing Coade stone in its original state with all the detailing clearly visible.*

An experienced fireman is a vital asset for any ceramics firm because all the work done stands or falls with the final firing. The comment about not using any thermometer is interesting as Josiah Wedgwood developed a pyrometer in 1783 for use in kilns and he is known to have sent one to John Bacon at the Coade factory. Bacon either did not give it to the fireman or the fireman chose not to use it.

Coade stone has a beautiful buff fired surface that weathers well and the modelling and detailing is usually still very crisp after all this time compared to stone statues and ornamentation of a similar date. Unfortunately many Coade stone artefacts have been covered in layers of paint and, although paint can add colour and gaiety, over time the piece becomes unsightly when the paint begins to peel. In general, Coade stone is best left in its original state.

Products and styles

The building of new country houses and the creation of park landscapes, as well as the building of large town houses in London, helped to create a market for Coade stone during the second half of the eighteenth century and the beginning of the nineteenth. Hand-carved stone ornamentation was always expensive and, although the cost of developing Coade stone prototypes (clay modelling and making plaster casts) was not cheap, once the moulds were made multiple copies could be produced at a fraction of the initial cost. For example, when in 1815 the committee of the New Bethlehem Hospital in Lambeth (now the Imperial War Museum) wanted a royal coat of arms over the main

Above: Town houses in Bedford Square, Bloomsbury, London, built c.1775, with Coade stone decorative features around the doors.

Royal coat of arms erected in 1815 over the entrance of the former New Bethlehem Hospital (now the Imperial War Museum), Lambeth, London, and stamped with the Coade mark, just visible beneath the lion.

A Coade stone Grecian sphinx at Gosford House, Longniddry, East Lothian.

entrance they opted for one made of Coade stone at a cost of 130 guineas rather than the same thing carved in Portland stone at a cost of £500.

Anything that could be carved in stone could also be made in Coade stone and, in view of the cost factor, it is not surprising that the range of Coade stone products was large. They made statues and busts, commemorative monuments and tombs, sculptures of lions and sphinxes, as well as garden ornaments such as fountains, vases, urns and

Below left: Coade stone ornamentation on the gateway at Easton Neston, Towcester, Northamptonshire.

Below right: Statue symbolising Meekness, marked and dated 'Coade Lambeth, 1790', in the vestibule of the chapel at the Old Royal Naval College, Greenwich.

pineapples. There was also a plethora of architectural detailing, including capitals for columns, keystones, coats of arms, paterae, balusters, string-courses, swags, chimneys, turrets and consoles as well as decorative plaques and roundels with classical figures and cherubs. For interior use decorative chimney-pieces were made, as well as candelabra, lamp and candle holders.

Some of the most interesting Coade stone products were funerary and commemorative monuments. Funerary monuments range from simple gravestones and weeping vestals draped over urns to large elaborate tombs. Tombs of particular interest are those of Admiral Bligh (Captain during the mutiny on the *Bounty*) in St Mary's churchyard, Lambeth; the monument to Lady Henniker at Rochester Cathedral, with the magnificent symbolic figure of Father Time holding his scythe and hourglass; and the grand militaristic tomb of Major General Bowes,

Coade stone tomb of Admiral Bligh in the churchyard of St Mary's Church (now the Museum of Garden History), Lambeth, London, 1826.

Tomb of Major General Bowes, who died in 1812 at the Battle of Salamanca, Spain, marked and dated 'Coade & Sealy, 1813', in Beverley Minster.

Coade stone statue of George III on the Esplanade in Weymouth, erected in 1809.

complete with cannons and cannonballs, in Beverley Minster.

Commemorative monuments of Coade stone include statues of royalty and other famous people, such as those of George III on the Esplanade at Weymouth and William Shakespeare outside Stratford Public Library in Newham, London, and the bust of the painter and writer James Barry in the crypt of St Paul's Cathedral in London. The less famous are sometimes also remembered, as for example the small plaque in honour of William Mason at All Saints' Church, Aston, South Yorkshire; he was a popular local poet and rector during the second half of the eighteenth century.

In a class of his own was Admiral Horatio Nelson, whose famous victory and heroic death at the Battle of Trafalgar in 1805 prompted the erection of many monuments in his honour; the Coade firm received commissions for several of them. At Great Yarmouth a Nelson monument was erected in 1819 in the form of a tall

Coade stone portrait of the poet William Mason, rector of All Saints' Church, Aston, South Yorkshire, marked and dated 'Coade & Sealy, 1804'.

The Nelson Column at Great Yarmouth with the statue of Britannia.

Doric column with the figure of Britannia (now replaced by a fibreglass replica) on top. A commission came from Montreal in Canada in 1809, also for a stone column with a Coade stone statue of Nelson. The greatest Nelson monument made of Coade stone is in King William Court at the Old Royal Naval College in Greenwich. It is in the form of an imposing pediment and is one of the finest achievements of the Coade factory in terms of size, modelling and execution. The pediment, dated 1812, was designed by Benjamin West and modelled with the assistance of Joseph Panzetta. It is 40 feet (12 metres) long and 10 feet (3 metres) high and shows Britannia receiving the dead body of Nelson from the sea-god Neptune with a host of attendant figures and animals on either side.

Coade products could be obtained in different styles, although much of what was produced was made in the classical style – or in the 'best Classical manner', as it was called then. The classical designs used by Coade reveal two main sources. The first are the classical forms derived from

The Nelson pediment in King William Court, Old Royal Naval College, Greenwich, 1809–12, with a fine array of Coade stone figures designed by Benjamin West and modelled by Joseph Panzetta.

The orangery at Burton Constable, East Yorkshire, designed by William Atkinson in 1788–9, decorated with Coade stone statues of Pomona, Ceres and Flora, pineapples, urns, figurative roundels and paterae.

Rome via the Renaissance and Baroque periods, which in the eighteenth century became known as the Palladian style in Britain. It is an elegant form of classicism filtered and refined over time. The porch with Coade stone sculptures at Schomberg House, Pall Mall, London, erected in 1791, and the orangery with Coade stone ornamentation at Burton Constable, East Yorkshire, built in 1788–9, are examples of this approach. With the exploits of Lord Elgin in Greece at the beginning of the nineteenth century and the eventual display of the so-called Elgin Marbles from the Parthenon in London in 1807, a new interest in Greek architecture and sculpture came about. The Coade factory, for example, made copies of the caryatids from the Erecteum in Athens, and the figures in the Nelson pediment at Greenwich show the direct influence of the Greek sculptures from the Parthenon.

Porch with Coade stone figures and a plaque with a reclining figure personifying the art of painting, at Schomberg House, Pall Mall, Westminster, London, 1791.

Coade stone caryatid in Greek dress on the façade of Sir John Soane's Museum, Lincoln's Inn Fields, Holborn, London.

Gothic ornamentation was also available on request. Coade products in this style often took the form of structural decorative components such as the Tudor fan vaulting of the screen in St George's Chapel at Windsor, the turrets, chimneys and battlements at Dalmeny House near Edinburgh and the Gothic archway at St Mary's churchyard at Tremadog in Gwynedd. The vogue for things in the Egyptian style that followed Napoleon's 1798 campaign in Egypt was also catered for. The pharaonic statues in the grounds of Buscot Park, Oxfordshire, and the Egyptian House in Penzance are examples of this trend. Even the exotic styles of Indian culture can be seen in Coade stone products such as the statue of the Hindu god Surya and the figures of Brahmin bulls at Sezincote, Gloucestershire.

Coade stone was also exported abroad and the Coade factory's books show that their products

An ornate Gothic archway entirely constructed of Coade stone at St Mary's Church, Tremadog, Gwynedd, 1811.

Above left: *An Egyptian-style Coade stone statue at Buscot Park, Oxfordshire, marked and dated 'Coade & Sealy, 1800'.*

Above right: *Coade stone statue of the Hindu sun-god Surya on a carriage drawn by seven horses in a specially designed garden temple at Sezincote, Gloucestershire, 1814.*

were sent not only to Ireland, the Netherlands and Gibraltar but also as far away as Russia, the United States of America, Canada, Brazil and even Haiti. There was a truly entrepreneurial spirit at the Coade factory and the overriding objective of the business was to provide their clients with exactly what they wanted.

The Coade stone monument to Timothy Brett erected in 1791 in the grounds of Mount Edgcumbe House, Cornwall.

Sculptors and architects

The high quality of the artistic modelling and design of Coade stone was another important factor in its success. Mrs Coade was able to attract the services of important sculptors and painters, among whom were John Bacon (1740–99), Thomas Banks (1735–1805), John Flaxman (1755–1826), John Charles Felix Rossi (1762–1839) and Benjamin West (1738–1820), all members of the Royal Academy.

Most of these had only occasional dealings with the Coade factory, but John Bacon, as we have already seen, joined the Coade firm in 1771 and worked there as full-time manager and 'in-house' artist until his death in 1799. Many of the designs for classical figures illustrated in the books of *Coade's Etchings* published in the 1770s and 1780s seem to be by his hand. In 1799, when the Coade Gallery was opened, a special pamphlet was published to mark the occasion and it refers to John Bacon's contribution to the firm: 'With no disparagement of others, many acknowledgements are due to the genius and exertions in the early years of its establishment of the late Mr Bacon, whose models now form a considerable part of its collection.' One of Bacon's most celebrated pieces for Coade was the large figure of the river-god Thames, which can still

Below left: *Coade stone figure of Father Time, attributed to Thomas Banks, on the monument to Lady Henniker in Rochester Cathedral, 1793.*

Below right: *Coade stone statue of Britannia, modelled by J. C. F. Rossi, on the roof of Liverpool Town Hall, c.1792.*

A 'bronzed' candlestick holder with the classical figure of Hymen, marked 'Coade Lambeth', designed by John Bacon, now at Heaton Hall, near Manchester.

be seen in front of Ham House near Richmond. Although much of his time was given to the Coade firm, Bacon occasionally did work for other ceramic manufacturers, such as Wedgwood in Stoke-on-Trent, but since their products were very different from Coade's it cannot be regarded as working for a rival firm.

The Coade firm also employed specialist modellers in clay. One such was Joseph Panzetta, who worked for Coade for many years. He helped to model the Nelson pediment at the Old Royal Naval College in Greenwich and was also responsible for the statue of Lord Hill (Lord Hill's Column) in Shrewsbury. John Sealy, Mrs Coade's business partner, also seems to have been an accomplished clay modeller. Richard Philips, in his *The Picture of London* (1804), noted that 'Mr Sealy has lately finished a colossal statue of his Majesty to be placed... at Weymouth', where it can still be admired today.

Detail of the expertly modelled river-god Thames at Ham House, Surrey, by John Bacon.

Lord Hill's Column, Abbey Foregate, Shrewsbury, erected in 1816. The Coade stone statue of Lord Hill was modelled by Joseph Panzetta.

Left: *20 Portman Square, Marylebone, London, designed by Robert Adam, 1775–7, with Coade stone embellishments in the form of oblong panels with swags and paterae, and guilloche string-courses.*

Equally important was Mrs Coade's acquaintance with many notable architects of the day, including Robert Adam (1728–92), James Wyatt (1746–1813), John Nash (1752–1835) and Sir John Soane (1753–1837). Many of Robert Adam's town and country houses have Coade stone as part of their ornamentation, among them 20 Portman Square in London, the Town Hall and Theatre in Bury St Edmunds, the Island Temple in Croome Park, Worcestershire, and in Scotland Culzean Castle in South Ayrshire and Castle Park Barracks, Dunbar, East Lothian. The grandest example is Gosford House in East Lothian, which

Gosford House, Longniddry, East Lothian, designed by Robert Adam, 1791–1800.

The Radcliffe Observatory, Oxford, designed by James Wyatt between 1772 and 1794 and decorated with Coade stone ornament modelled by J. C. F. Rossi.

Adam had designed for the Earl of Wemyss in 1791, but which was not completed until 1800. Although there is Coade stone ornament on the main house, the greatest concentration is found on the stable block, an independent group of small buildings set well away from the house. Here the visitor is met by a rich array of Coade stone in the form of sphinxes and small lions on the roof, medallions and plaques with classical figures on the façade and large plaques with figures representing the Arts and Agriculture above every door in the stable yard. Even the stone boathouse near the lake is decorated with Coade stone.

James Wyatt was one of the most prominent architects of his day, even rivalling Robert Adam. An early example of his work was Heaton Hall (1772) near Manchester, where he used Coade stone capitals, paterae and string-courses. He became involved with the building of the Radcliffe Observatory in Oxford in 1772, which continued until 1794. Here much Coade stone ornamentation was used, including signs of the zodiac and plaques with scenes from classical mythology designed by J. C. F. Rossi.

Panel on the exterior of the Radcliffe Observatory, Oxford, showing the sun-god Helios streaking along the sky in his horse-drawn chariot.

Guardhouse in the Greek style on the west side of Buckingham Palace, designed by John Nash between 1826 and 1830, surmounted by an elaborate Coade stone coat of arms flanked by the lion and unicorn.

When Wyatt reconstructed Liverpool Town Hall in 1780–92, he was again collaborating with Rossi, who modelled the large and imposing Coade stone figure of Britannia on the roof.

John Nash obtained a number of royal commissions such as the garden ornamentation for the Royal Lodge, Windsor, for which he ordered copies of Coade's Borghese and Medici vases placed on specially designed Coade stone pedestals. He was also occupied with the building of Buckingham Palace from 1826 until the death of George IV in 1830. He commissioned the Coade factory to make such decorative features as figurative friezes designed by John Flaxman, coats of arms for the guardhouses, capitals, statues and vases for the gardens.

The architect who had the longest association with the Coade factory was Sir John Soane. One of his earliest commissions was a gateway combined with lodges at Langley Park, Norfolk (1784), where he used Coade stone paterae and chimneys. Soane is best known for his work as the Surveyor to the Bank of England (1788–1833), in which he used a great deal of Coade stone decoration. One of his most striking creations at the Bank was Lothbury Court, which had four massive projecting Corinthian columns topped with Coade stone statues representing the four continents. He also used this specific architectural device for his own house, Pitzhanger Manor in Ealing (1800–3), which is fronted by four tall projecting Ionic columns, topped by Greek caryatids. Two Coade stone caryatids can also be found on the exterior of what is now Sir John Soane's Museum in Lincoln's Inn Fields, London. This consists of three adjoining town houses that Soane acquired over the period from 1792 to 1823 for use as a family home and repository for his vast collection of books and antique architectural decorations and statues. Soane owned a book containing etchings of Coade stone designs that has remained in his library to this day.

Not only architects used Coade stone: landscape designers, too, made use of the material in the form of ornamental features to adorn their parks, a surviving example being the work of 'Capability' Brown at Croome Park in Worcestershire.

Although many examples of Coade stone have survived, much of it goes unrecognised because it is often mistaken for real stone. A trained

The façade of Pitzhanger Manor, Ealing, London, designed by Sir John Soane in 1800–3 with Coade stone caryatids on top of the Ionic columns.

eye, however, will spot that Coade stone has weathered better than the surrounding stonework, and the modelling and detailing of Coade stone will often be as sharp as on the day it was made. The greatest problem in identifying Coade stone arises when it has been covered with several layers of paint. This makes it unrecognisable and in these instances one has to rely on documentary evidence such as factory records. However, seeking out Coade stone is a rewarding and interesting pursuit, especially when marked and dated examples are discovered. It is not only an exercise in reclaiming an important part of the decorative architectural heritage of the late eighteenth and early nineteenth centuries but it also honours the memory of a very remarkable Georgian businesswoman.

Places to visit

There are still many places throughout Britain where Coade stone can be seen and most of them are listed by Alison Kelly in her book *Mrs Coade's Stone* (1990). However, many of these locations are not publicly accessible or are difficult to find, while others have now completely disappeared. The following list is a representative selection of Coade stone locations in Britain and Ireland that are still extant. Coade stone examples in public places can be seen all the year around, but those at National Trust properties, country houses open to the public, museums, churches and cathedrals can be seen only at certain times, and opening times should be ascertained before travelling.

ENGLAND
BERKSHIRE
Windsor
   Windsor Castle: Coade stone screen with fan vaulting in St George's Chapel and three Coade stone statues on the west front of the chapel, 1799.

BUCKINGHAMSHIRE
Buckingham
   London Road Bridge (over the river Great Ouse): the coat of arms of the Marquess of Buckingham on the east side, marked and dated 'Coade & Sealy, Lambeth, 1805'; on the west side a plaque with the swan of Buckingham, marked 'Coade & Sealy, 1809'.

High Wycombe
   Guildhall: Coade stone coat of arms in the pediment.

Coat of arms of the Marquess of Buckingham on London Road Bridge spanning the river Great Ouse in Buckingham, marked and dated 'Coade & Sealy, 1805'.

An imposing Coade stone lion at Stowe, Buckinghamshire.

Stowe

Stowe House and Landscape Gardens (National Trust): Coade stone lion, Coade stone plaques and chimneys on the lodges at the Buckingham end of the Grand Avenue; the Oxford lodges have Coade stone coats of arms.

Taplow

Taplow Court (Historic Houses Association): urns on gate piers and statue of George III in Roman dress in front of the house, marked 'Coade & Sealy, 1804'.

CORNWALL
Mount Edgcumbe

Mount Edgcumbe House and Country Park: triangular Coade stone monument, 14 feet (4.3 metres) high and standing on three stone tortoises; it was erected in 1791 by Admiral George Edgcumbe to commemorate his friend Timothy Brett.

Penzance

Egyptian House, Chapel Street: façade heavily enriched with Coade stone ornament, including Egyptian figures and winged serpents, *c.*1835.

Truro

Assembly Rooms and Theatre: Coade stone medallions of Garrick and Shakespeare and plaques with a muse and a pair of griffins, 1772.

CUMBRIA
Great Corby

Corby Castle (a medieval Scottish tower

The Egyptian House with colourfully painted Coade stone decorations, Chapel Street, Penzance, c.1835.

house rebuilt in the early nineteenth century): pele tower with Coade stone bas-relief showing Apollo and two medallions depicting earth and water, Coade stone lions on the roof, 1815; gate lodge with medallion showing Diana, 1818. The castle can be seen from the footpath on the east side of the river Eden.

DEVON
Bicton Park
Orangery: busts of Nelson, Sir Walter Raleigh and Wellington, marked and dated 'Coade & Sealy, 1806'.

Exeter
Wyvern Barracks: royal coat of arms, marked and dated 'Coade & Sealy, 1806'.
Southernhay East and West: terraces with numerous Coade stone keystones over front doors.

DORSET
Dewlish
All Saints' churchyard: headstone of Charles Hill, marked and dated 'Coade London, 1792'.

Lyme Regis
Belmont (eighteenth-century house on the corner of Pound Street and Cobb Road): in 1784 Eleanor Coade took over the lease on this house and decorated it with products of her factory.

Weymouth
Esplanade: statue of George III, erected in 1809.

ESSEX
Chelmsford
Moulsham Bridge: Coade stone head of river-god and paterae, 1787.
Shire Hall, Magistrates' Court, Tindal Square: Coade stone plaques of Wisdom, Mercy and

Lunette on the gravestone of Charles Hill in All Saints' churchyard, Dewlish, Dorset, marked 'Coade London, 1792'.

Monument to George III on the Esplanade in Weymouth, erected in 1809. The Coade stone statues of the king and the lion and unicorn at the base have been richly painted.

Justice on the façade and a Coade stone naiad (water nymph) on a fountain decorated with dolphins in the corner of the entrance hall, 1789–91.

Harwich
   St Nicholas's Church, Church Street: Coade stone Gothic pinnacles on the roof, 1821.

GLOUCESTERSHIRE
Sezincote
   Sezincote House (Historic Houses Association): Temple Pool with Coade stone statue of the Indian god Surya, flanked by two Indian bulls, marked 'Coade London, 1814'; also Borghese vase marked 'Coade Lambeth'.

An Indian bull at Sezincote, Gloucestershire, marked and dated 'Coade London, 1814'.

Stow-on-the-Wold
St Edward's Church: Coade stone urn in memory of Leonard Hayward, 1780.

HAMPSHIRE
Farleigh Wallop
Farleigh House: gate piers with Coade stone mermaids, 1780–5.

Sherborne St John
The Vyne (National Trust): Coade stone druid in the grounds.

Southampton
Bargate: Coade statue of George III in Roman dress in a niche, marked and dated 'Coade & Sealy, 1809'.

HERTFORDSHIRE
Langley
St Lawrence's Church: Coade stone shields with the arms of England in the porch, 1814.

Watton-at-Stone
Woodhall Park: Coade stone plaques with crossed arrows and cornucopia, consoles to ground-floor windows and Ionic capitals, 1785 (grant-aided by English Heritage).

KENT
Broadstairs
Nuckell's Almshouse, High Street, St Peter's in Thanet: a figure of Charity in a niche over the door, marked 'Coade Lambeth'.

The façade of Nuckell's Almshouse, dated 1838, in the High Street of St Peter's in Thanet, Broadstairs, Kent, with a statue of Charity marked 'Coade Lambeth' in a niche above the door.

The richly painted royal coat of arms over the main entrance of Chatham Historic Dockyard, marked and dated 'Coade & Sealy, 1812'.

Chatham

Chatham Historic Dockyard: a large royal coat of arms over the main entrance gate, marked and dated 'Coade & Sealy, 1812'.

Cobham

Cobham Hall (Historic Houses Association): Coade stone Borghese and Medici vases in the gardens on the west front, 1801.

Rochester

Rochester Cathedral: monument to Lady Henniker flanked on one side by a figure of Father Time and on the other by an angel; the angel is marked and dated 'Coade London 1793'.

Throwley

Belmont (Historic Houses Association): Coade stone plaques with swags and the Four Seasons on the façade, 1792.

LANCASHIRE

Lancaster

Royal Infirmary, Ashton Road: re-sited over the main entrance is a Coade stone plaque depicting the story of the Good Samaritan, taken from the demolished Town Dispensary (1785).

Right: Coade stone statues of an angel and Father Time flank the Henniker monument in Rochester Cathedral. The figure of the angel is marked and dated 'Coade London, 1793'.

A Coade stone plaque depicting the story of the Good Samaritan. Originally at the former Town Dispensary (1785) in Lancaster, it is now set over the main door of Lancaster Royal Infirmary.

One of the Ionic capitals made of Coade stone on the façade of Heaton Hall, near Manchester, designed by James Wyatt in 1772.

Liverpool
Town Hall: colossal Coade stone statue of Britannia on the dome, 1792.

Manchester
Heaton Hall, Heaton Park (Manchester City Council): stone column and pilasters on the façade topped by Coade stone capitals, paterae and string-courses, 1772.

LINCOLNSHIRE
Bloxholm
St Michael's Church: arms of General Manners over the entrance porch, marked and dated 'Coade & Sealy, 1813'.

Lincoln
Lincoln Castle: Coade stone bust of George III in the grounds, 1810.

LONDON
Belgravia
Norwegian Embassy, 25 Belgrave Square: panels on the exterior with cherubs engaged in various kinds of pursuits, 1796.

Bloomsbury
Bedford Square: houses with Coade stone keystones over front doors, *c.*1775.

Above: *Close-up of a cherub personifying the art of painting on the outside wall of the Norwegian Embassy, Belgrave Square, Belgravia, London, 1796. It is part of a bigger Coade stone panel representing the arts.*

Left: *A Coade stone bust of George III in the grounds of Lincoln Castle.*

A Coade stone keystone above the doors of one of the houses in Bedford Square, Bloomsbury, London.

City of London
St Paul's Cathedral: Coade stone bust of James Barry, 1819, in the crypt.

Ealing
Pitzhanger Manor, Mattock Lane: Coade stone caryatids perched on columns on the façade; inside there are caryatids in the Breakfast Room and Eating Room, 1800–3.

Finsbury
Bunhill Fields Cemetery, City Road: tomb of the Reverend Henry Hunter, marked 'Coade & Sealy, 1801'.

Greenwich
Old Royal Naval College, Romney Road: the Nelson Pediment in King William Court has an elaborate Coade stone sculpture arrangement showing Britannia receiving the dead body of Nelson from the sea-god Neptune, dated 1812. The chapel of St Peter and St Paul has Coade stone decorations and statues added in stages between 1779 and 1789; in the vestibule are four statues representing Hope, Faith, Charity and Meekness; in the chapel Coade stone pilasters and bases for capitals, cherub heads, medallions with

The Coade stone tomb of the Reverend Henry Hunter, surmounted by an obelisk, in Bunhill Fields Cemetery, Finsbury, London.

Left: *Detail of the Nelson pediment at the Old Royal Naval College, Greenwich, showing Britannia receiving the body of Nelson.*

Right: *A Coade stone roundel showing the Conversion of St Paul, one of a series depicting the life of St Paul on the pulpit in the chapel at the Old Royal Naval College, Greenwich.*

prophets and apostles and the hospital arms; round plaques with scenes from the life of St Paul on the pulpit, and the communion table is supported by gilded Coade stone angels.

Holborn
Sir John Soane's Museum, Lincoln's Inn Fields: caryatids on the façade, c.1825.

Lambeth
Imperial War Museum, Lambeth Road: royal coat of arms over the main entrance, marked and dated 'Coade, 1815'.

St Mary's Church (now the Museum of Garden History), Lambeth Palace Road: Coade stone tombs of the Sealy family and Admiral Bligh.

Westminster Bridge (Lambeth side): Coade stone lion on pedestal, dated 1837.

Marylebone
20–21 Portman Square: decorated with Coade stone ornament, 1775.

Wimpole Street: many houses on either side have Coade stone keystones over the front doors, c.1775.

Above: *A Coade stone keystone of a bearded man at 10 Wimpole Street, Marylebone, London, c.1775.*

Left: *The Coade stone tomb of the Sealy family in front of St Mary's Church, Lambeth, London, 1800.*

Newham

Romford Road, Stratford: Coade stone statue of Shakespeare outside public library, 1816–18.

Paddington

St Mary's Church, Paddington Green: vestal with an urn (monument to Joseph Johnson) in a niche on the exterior of the south wall, marked and dated 'Coade & Sealy, 1802'.

Westminster

Buckingham Palace, The Mall: Coade stone friezes around inner courtyard, coats of arms on guardhouses, vases in the gardens, 1826–30.

Westminster Abbey: Coade stone monument to Edward Wortley Montagu, on the west wall of the cloister near the door to the Abbey, 1777.

Schomberg House, 80–82 Pall Mall: porch with Coade stone figures and a plaque, 1791.

The monument to Joseph Johnson, St Mary's Church, Paddington Green, London, marked and dated 'Coade & Sealy, 1802'.

The Coade stone memorial dedicated to Edward Wortley Montagu, in the cloister of Westminster Abbey, London, 1777.

NORFOLK
Great Yarmouth
Nelson Column: statue of Britannia (fibreglass copy) on top of column with six caryatids, 1819.

Loddon
Langley Park: neo-classical gatehouse with Coade stone paterae and small chimneys, 1784.

NORTHAMPTONSHIRE
Desborough
St Giles's Church: Coade stone monument to Mrs Pulton, 1779.

Towcester
Easton Neston estate: ornamental gateway with screens (now entrance to Towcester Racecourse) decorated with capitals, coat of arms, vases and sculptures of hinds, many marked and dated 'Croggon late Coade, London, 1822'.

NORTHUMBERLAND
Alnwick
Tenantry Column: erected by the Duke of Northumberland's tenants, with four large Coade stone lions at the base, 1816.

Gateway at Langley Park, Loddon, Norfolk, with Coade stone paterae and chimneys by Sir John Soane, 1784.

Gateway with screens at Easton Neston, Towcester, Northamptonshire, designed by John Raffield, richly decorated with various kinds of Coade stone ornament, much of it marked and dated 'Croggon late Coade, London, 1822'.

Ponteland

Parish church: memorial to Richard Newton Ogle, marked 'Coade, 1799'.

OXFORDSHIRE

Buscot

Buscot Park (National Trust): two Egyptian figures in the grounds, marked and dated 'Coade & Sealy, Lambeth, 1800'.

One of the Coade stone lions at the base of the Tenantry Column, Alnwick, Northumberland, 1816.

Coade stone sign of the zodiac (Aries) by J. C. F. Rossi at the Radcliffe Observatory, Oxford.

Oxford
Radcliffe Observatory, Green College: Coade stone decorations in the form of pilaster capitals, paterae, roundels and the signs of the zodiac. In between the zodiac signs on the north side are three Coade stone panels representing Morning, Noon and Evening, 1772–94.

SHROPSHIRE
Shrewsbury
Lord Hill's Column, Abbey Foregate: Coade stone statue of Lord Hill on a 100 feet (30 metres) high Doric column erected in 1816.

STAFFORDSHIRE
Shugborough
Shugborough House (National Trust): portico with Ionic columns with Coade stone capitals in front of the house; Coade stone antefix at the back of the house; a statue of a druid situated near the river; a Coade stone plaque on the Cat's Monument on a small island in the gardens; also two gate lodges with coats of arms, one marked 'Croggon, London, 1824'.

One of the gate lodges at the entrance to the Shugborough estate in Staffordshire, decorated with the coat of arms of the Earl of Lichfield, marked and dated 'Croggon, London, 1824'.

The Market Hall and Theatre in Cornhill, Bury St Edmunds, designed by Robert Adam and decorated with Coade stone urns, swags, paterae and capitals, 1775–8.

SUFFOLK
Bury St Edmunds
Market Hall and Theatre, Cornhill: niches with Coade stone urns, swags, paterae and Ionic capitals, 1775–8.

Ickworth
Ickworth House (National Trust): small section of the upper frieze with Coade stone figures at the back of the house, installed in the 1820s.

SURREY
Chertsey
St Peter's Church: aisles rebuilt in 1806–8 with Coade stone tracery for the windows and window label stops with a variety of different designs.

Ham
Ham House (National Trust): Coade stone statue of the river-god Thames in front of the house, and garden railings with twelve pineapples, marked and dated 'Coade & Sealy, 1800' or '1801'.

Detail of the Coade stone frieze on Ickworth House, Suffolk, designed by Mario Asprucci, 1795–1803. The frieze based on Flaxman's designs illustrating Homer's 'Iliad' and 'Odyssey' was not added until the 1820s.

Far left: *The Medici vase at Kew Gardens, marked and dated 'Croggon, Lambeth, 1826'; it was previously at the Royal Lodge gardens at Windsor.*

Left: *One of the pineapples on the garden railings at Ham House, Surrey, marked and dated 'Coade & Sealy, Lambeth, 1800'.*

Kew

Kew Gardens: Coade stone Medici vase on a pedestal, north of the Palm House on the left-hand side of the pond, marked and dated 'Croggon, Lambeth, 1826'.

SUSSEX
Arundel

Arundel Castle: Coade stone horse and lion near the Norman castle mound, one stamped '1798'.

Chichester

Butter Market, North Street: Coade stone coat of arms of the city on the roof, marked 'Coade & Sealy, 1808'.

A finely modelled Coade stone horse (1798) at Arundel Castle, West Sussex.

The city's coat of arms on the roof of the Butter Market in Chichester, marked and dated 'Coade & Sealy, 1808'.

Petworth

Petworth House (National Trust): Coade stone fountain with Triton blowing a horn in the park, 1809.

St Mary's Church: Coade stone royal coat of arms, marked and dated 'Coade & Sealy, 1812' (now in the church meeting room).

Uppark

Uppark (National Trust): Coade stone Borghese vase in the grounds, c.1805.

Worthing

Castle Goring: the south façade has three Coade stone plaques showing Bacchus, Ceres and a satyr, 1790.

WORCESTERSHIRE
Croome Park

Croome Park (National Trust): Island Temple with Coade stone plaques of the Aldobrandini Marriage and a Phrygian shepherd and shepherdess, plus two panels with gryphons; statues of a druid and naiad in the park grounds and Coade stone heads on Dry Arch Bridge, 1797.

Coade stone Borghese vase with finely modelled classical figures at Uppark, West Sussex.

Keystone on Dry Arch Bridge at Croome Park, Worcestershire, marked and dated 'Coade London, 1797'.

Right: *Brightly painted Coade stone royal coat of arms in the pediment of Sessions House, New Walk, Beverley, 1807.*

YORKSHIRE, EAST
Beverley
Beverley Minster: tomb of Major General Bowes, marked and dated 'Coade & Sealy, 1813'.
Sessions House, New Walk: royal coat of arms in the pediment, 1807.

Burton Constable
Burton Constable Hall (Historic Houses Association): orangery with Coade stone statues and roundels, 1788–9.

Coade stone panel depicting Seafaring and Navigation on the façade of Sledmere House, near Driffield, East Yorkshire, designed by John Carr and Samuel Wyatt, 1782–90.

Section of the roofscape of Dalmeny House near Edinburgh, designed by William Wilkins Junior in 1814–17 with an array of Coade stone chimneys, turrets, battlements and string-courses.

Sledmere
Sledmere House (Historic Houses Association): plaques with classical figures and coat of arms, one panel marked and dated 'Coade London, 1789'.

YORKSHIRE, SOUTH
Aston
All Saints' Church: plaque commemorating the rector and poet William Mason, marked and dated 'Coade & Sealy, 1804'.

YORKSHIRE, WEST
Leeds
Temple Newsam (Leeds City Council): Coade stone copy of the Borghese vase, *c.*1790.

SCOTLAND
CITY OF EDINBURGH
Dalmeny
Dalmeny House (Historic Houses Association): Coade stone battlements, turrets and chimneys in the Tudor style, 1814–17.

EAST LOTHIAN
Dunbar
Castle Park Barracks (originally Dunbar Castle), at north end of High Street: Coade stone sphinx on the roof, 1790–2.

Coade stone sphinx on top of Castle Park Barracks, Dunbar, East Lothian, designed by Robert Adam, 1790–2.

Above left: *Coade stone coat of arms of the Wemyss family on the roof of Gosford House, Longniddry, East Lothian.*

Above right: *The stable block at Gosford House, festooned with Coade stone decorations.*

Haddington

Bank of Scotland (former villa), 44 High Street: a small Coade stone sphinx on the cornice and rectangular plaques with classical figures on the wings, 1802.

Longniddry

Gosford House (Historic Houses Association): the main house has a Coade stone portrait medallion of the Earl of Wemyss on the façade, as well as the family coat of arms, lions and sphinxes; the stables have Coade stone in the form of small sphinxes, lions, plaques and roundels with classical heads and figures; the boathouse on the lake also features Coade stone ornamentation (some of it damaged), 1791–1800.

MIDLOTHIAN
Pathhead

Preston Hall (2 miles north of Pathhead): entrance gates with Coade stone lions, *c.*1794.

SOUTH AYRSHIRE
Culzean

Culzean Castle (National Trust for Scotland): the Cat Gates have piers with Egyptian lionesses, one marked and dated 'Coade Lambeth, 1802', and Coade stone coats of arms over two garden archways.

Coade stone lion on the entrance gates of Preston Hall, Pathhead, Midlothian.

Two grotesque faces on the Gothic archway at St Mary's Church, Tremadog, Gwynedd.

The Duke of Richmond's Fountain, Merrion Square, Dublin, designed by H. A. Baker, 1791, decorated with Coade stone plaques, roundels and urns.

Rotunda Hospital, Parnell Street, Dublin, designed by James Gandon, 1786, decorated with Coade stone ox skulls and drapery.

WALES
GWYNEDD
Tremadog
St Mary's Church: ornamental Coade stone archway in the Gothic style at the entrance to the churchyard, 1811.

Town Hall, Market Square: Coade stone medallions and keystones on the façade.

IRELAND
Dublin
Amiens Street: Lord Aldborough's House has a Coade stone coat of arms, swags, lions and sphinxes on the roof, 1793–8.

Eccles Street: house of the architect Francis Johnston (1760–1829), with Coade stone plaques on the façade.

Merrion Square: Duke of Richmond's Fountain, decorated with Coade stone urns, plaques and roundels, 1791.

Parnell Street: Rotunda Hospital has a frieze below the dome decorated with Coade stone ox skulls and drapery with square decorative panels below, 1786.

Further reading

Kelly, Alison. 'Sir John Soane and Mrs Eleanor Coade', *Apollo*, April 1989.

Kelly, Alison. *Mrs Coade's Stone.* The Self Publishing Association, 1990.

Kelly, Alison. 'Coade stone: its character and conservation', in *Architectural Ceramics.* English Heritage, 1996.

Ruch, John. 'Regency Coade: a study of the Coade record books, 1813–21', *Architectural History*, volume 11, 1968.

Stratton, Michael. *The Terracotta Revival.* Gollancz, 1993.

Coade stone vase on the gateway at Easton Neston, Towcester, Northamptonshire.

Coade stone coat of arms of the town on the façade of the eighteenth-century Guildhall, High Street, High Wycombe, Buckinghamshire.

Index